In the Kitchen with Nan

©2008 by Regina Flemion

Published by American Imaging
Cover design: Jim Grich
Format and packaging: Peggy Grich

All rights reserved worldwide. No parts of the contents of this book may be reproduced or transmitted in any form by any means without the permission of the author.

First Edition 2008

ISBN 978-1-60702-589-4

In the Kitchen with Nan

**by
Regina (Nan) Flemion**

Favorite Recipes
From Nan's Cookbook

Recipe Name	Page Number

Table of Contents

Introduction 1

Soups, Salads, Breads 7

Fish 22

Main Dishes, Vegetables 24

Casseroles 40

Fruits and Desserts 45

Recipe Index 56

Brown Velvet Coat

I remember a brown velvet coat my Grandmother Lynch made for me. I felt like a princess in it. It wasn't very often I had something new that wasn't handed down about three times. I remember a doll I got from a basket that was delivered to our house around Christmas time. We didn't have many toys but we did have a lot of love. We had balls, jump ropes, jacks, pick-up sticks, and we played hopscotch. All the kids played in the alley a few doors down from were we lived at 1129 Montello Avenue, N.E., in Washington, D.C. I was born in that house and they say my first bed was a dresser drawer. Easter and Christmas were special times. They were wonderful family gatherings with lots of food and presents. My mom and dad went to a lot of trouble to get a Christmas tree on Christmas Eve and decorate it before Christmas morning. Back then everything was done on Christmas Eve. I guess that was because it wasn't as elaborate as it is now.

    My dad always waited until Christmas Eve as trees were not as expensive then. Sometimes they even gave them away. My dad worked at Topham's Trunk Factory. At times there was extra fabric leftover from making the trunks and my dad would bring it home to make drapes. One year he made everything my brother John's daughter, Charlotte, received for Christmas except for a doll. This was during World War II. He made her a table and chair set with a kitchen cabinet that had drawers and glass doors like a real china cabinet; a rocking chair; a rocking horse; and a two-seater swing.

    I remember the smallest grandchild would sit on his lap at the dinner table and eat from his plate. I also remember making ice cream with snow, sugar and milk. Some days in the winter were so cold that we would sit on the radiators to keep warm. Easter Monday we had a family picnic and my Grandmother Lynch would fill our baskets before we all left to go roll our eggs. Sometimes we would go to the Capital or the Washington Monument or Lincoln Park for the egg rolling. For a real treat, we would go to North Beach on Sundays. My mom and dad and Grandmother Ward loved to play the slot machines. The kids would go swimming. It's a wonder we didn't drown as none of us could swim.

I loved taking lunch to my dad at his work. He made the luggage I took on my honeymoon. I can't think of much I didn't like about my mom and dad. They were wonderful parents. They gave us lots of love and took good care of us. We always had a roof over our heads and food to eat. My dad would pick up a penny and say ninety-nine more would make a dollar. I think of him every time I find a penny. It's hard to think of a characteristic that I didn't like about my mom and dad. They didn't have much to give us but they gave us all they had. People would say, "If you knew my dad you loved him." I didn't like my mom smoking. I can't think of anything else. She was a wonderful loving person. I didn't like it when my dad would tell us what was in the food we were eating.

My oldest brother, John, was very good to me and tried to help me. He would tell me to brush my teeth and hold my shoulders back. After he and Evelyn were married, I lived with them before the war started. They sent me to school and clothed me. We lived just a few blocks from where my dad worked. I took him his lunch and there was an alleyway where I could climb up on the window ledge and talk to him while he ate his lunch. Then Charlotte, John's daughter, was born. The war started and John was sent to Germany. I was only about ten then and that's when my babysitting began.

Some people came to our door one year at Christmas time. They came to deliver a huge basket full of food and fruit and a baby doll. I took the doll from the basket for myself. I don't remember who brought it or where it came from. My brothers, John and Fritz, were embarrassed by it and they hid in one of the back rooms. John was proud and didn't like handouts. He had a lot of ambition and pride. Even to this day, he wants everything he has to be the best. So far, I think he's accomplished his goal.

My sister, Harolyn (Sissy), was like a mother hen. She took care of all of us until she got married and left home. It seemed like when one would leave the next one in line would take over the chores. Sissy was so pretty. She had beautiful black hair and was in love with a Marine. She wanted to marry him, but my parents thought she was too young.

My brother, Elwood (Fritz), had a heart of gold. He loved everyone and would do anything he could to help you. He worked hard all of his life as a bricklayer. He liked to work with his hands building things. I remember his and John's job was to shovel the coal from the street to the basement and sometimes I would help. One time, Fritz was delivering papers and got bit by a dog. I remember a policeman coming to the house and they took him to the hospital. I remember he and John played baseball in the alley and I remember someone hit John in the head with a brick. Our next door neighbors took him to the hospital because mom and dad weren't at home. Our neighbors were really nice people. They were colored. That's what they were called then. Fritz was sent to war, too. He was stationed in Italy. As always, he liked to do things for people, so he became a medic on the front lines. He got shot and received the Purple Heart and many other medals. When they delivered the news it was the first time I ever saw my dad cry. We were all thankful when he and John came home and the war was over.

John bought one of the first televisions. All they had on at that time was *The Milton Berle Show* and wrestling. We all gathered around every evening and watched whatever was on. Duke and I had our first date March 16, 1946. It was Fritz's wedding day. I was babysitting about five kids.

My sister, Josephine (Suggie, pronounced Shuggie): I remember she took Tinky (my youngest sister) and me to the Washington Monument on July 4th one year. I don't remember too much about it but we got into a lot of trouble. My mom was waiting for us when we got home because it was pretty late. They used to have a lot of movie stars at the fire works. I don't remember who was there. I remember wearing Suggie's shoes. They were too big for me so I stuffed toilet paper in the toes. I remember she had a big beautiful wedding; and I remember my mom had a seizure and had to be carried out of the church. She was in bed the rest of the night and wasn't able to go to the reception.

    My sister, Bernadine (Tinky): We had a fun, crazy life together. We fought a lot. I was the ambitious one and she was the baby of the family. I used to try and get her to help with the dishes or with cleaning the house but it was pretty hard to get her to do anything she didn't want to do. What a temper she had! She would sit in the middle of the street screaming and kicking her feet if she didn't get her way. She was sure stubborn. Sissy would get so mad at her. When my mother came home from work Tinky would run to meet her and tell her how badly I treated her. She was a little terror but as we grew up we became pretty good friends. She was the cutest little girl with bright red hair. My mother would curl her hair and put on a pretty dress and she would sing and dance on the stage at the movies. Every so often they would have amateur night and she would always win because she was so cute.

    I remember my Grandmother Ward. She was a very generous and good person. She must have been pretty well off at one time. She had a grocery store but I don't remember ever seeing it. She also had three husbands whom she buried. I don't remember any of them either. She took in and raised her son's five children after his wife left him and took everything but the children. I used to go visit her with my dad and he would always slip her some money to help her. I didn't like the fact that she was so superstitious. Sometimes she scared us all to death.

It's wonderful to have these memories to cherish. Long after they're gone, the people we love linger in our hearts. I hope you all celebrate Christmas by setting it apart as a special time for family, to reflect on how blessed we are and how amazing God's love is for each and every one of us. Merry Christmas! Enjoy *In the Kitchen with Nan*, and these many recipes whose main ingredient was love.

Nan

Soups, Salads, Breads

Duke's Favorite Bean Soup

¾ cup navy beans
¾ oz. onions
1-1/4 cup cold water
1-1/2 tsp. bacon fat
¼ cup celery
1-1/2 qt. cold water
1/3 tsp. salt
dash black pepper
1/8 tsp. dry mustard
¾ tsp. Worcestershire sauce
½ cup tomatoes w/juice
1/8 tsp. hot sauce
1 tbsp. plus 1 tsp. soup base
1-1/2 oz. ham
2 potatoes
¼ oz. roux

Cook for several hours and thicken with the roux (mix a little oil, flour and water in pan until the mixture thickens and add to soup).

Clam Chowder

5 potatoes
1 stalk celery/or cream of celery soup
1 large onion
4 tbsp. butter
4 cups milk
1 doz. clams with juice
fatback
salt and pepper

Dice first three ingredients. Dice and sauté fatback in butter, simmer until vegetables are soft. Add clams w/juice and heat. Do not boil.

Vegetable Soup

1 lb. ground beef or ham bone w/meat
1 large can tomatoes
1 can beef broth
1/2 cup water
2 cans green beans
1 pkg. frozen peas
1 pkg. frozen carrots
1 large onion, chopped
1 clove garlic minced
2 stalks celery, chopped
4 medium potatoes, cubed
salt and pepper to taste
Mrs. Dash's to taste

Brown ground beef; drain and add to remaining ingredients and cook for several hours.

Yummy Baked Beans

1 lb ground beef
1/2 to 1 cup onion finely chopped
2 cans (16-18 oz each) pork and beans
1/2 cup catsup
1/2 cup light Molasses
1 Tbsp spiced mustard
2 tsps Wright's natural hickory seasoning
few drops of red pepper sauce
garlic to taste

Crumble and cook beef, drain. Sauté onion. Put all ingredients in pot, heat until bubbling. Turn down and simmer at least 30 minutes uncovered, stirring occasionally. You can also cook them in a crockpot on low, overnight.

Cole Slaw

1 1-pound head cabbage, chopped well
2 large carrots, finely chopped
1 small onion, finely chopped
Mayonnaise or Miracle Whip to desired consistency
1 tablespoon sugar
salt to taste

You can either use a food processor or chop them all by hand.
Place the cabbage, carrots and onion in a large mixing bowl and add the mayonnaise or miracle whip to desired consistency. Then add the sugar and salt to taste. Chill before serving.

Corn Pudding

2 eggs
¼ cup sugar
1 cup milk
2 tbsp. butter
½ tsp. cornstarch
½ tsp. salt
1-1/2 cup crushed corn
sprinkle pepper on top

Mix above ingredients and bake in a greased dish for 40-45 minutes at 400 degrees.

Flemion Salad

Head of lettuce
4 green onions
1 cucumber
3 tomatoes (cubed)

Mix salt and pepper with miracle whip for the dressing

Manhattan Deli Salad

1-12 oz pkg. spiral pasta
1 cup chopped red or green pepper
1 small red onion cut in rings
1/4 cup chopped parsley
1/2 cup pitted ripe olives, sliced (Optional)
1/4 lb hard salami in thin strips
1/2 cup grated Parmesan cheese
3/4 cup Italian salad dressing

Cook pasta and drain. Mix next six ingredients with the pasta. Add dressing and toss prior to serving. If you add the dressing too early the pasta will absorb it all, so wait until you're ready to serve it.

Picnic Pineapple Slaw

12 cups shredded slaw
4 cups (2 cans) drained chunk pineapple
1 1/2 lbs (about 3) sliced bananas (into pineapple juice)
10 1/2 oz. Pkg. mini marshmallows

Dressing:
1 1/2 cup mayonnaise
1/4 cup sugar
1/4 cup pineapple juice

Mix all ingredients with dressing prior to serving so the bananas are still fresh and the marshmallows do not become mush.

Potato Salad

3-4 lbs potatoes, cooked, peeled and cubed
1 onion, chopped
3 stalks celery, chopped
1/4 cup mayonnaise or salad dressing
1 tablespoon prepared mustard
3 hard-cooked eggs
1/4 cup sweet pickle cubes or dill pickle cubes
Salt and pepper to taste
In large bowl, combine all ingredients except eggs, toss lightly. Top with sliced eggs and sprinkle with paprika. Chill until served.

Seven Layer Salad

1 head of lettuce, shredded
1/4 cup celery, chopped
1 green pepper, chopped
1 small onion, chopped
10 oz. pkg. frozen peas
2 cups Miracle Whip
2 tbs. sugar
4 strips bacon, cooked and diced
1/2 lb. cheddar cheese, grated

Cook and drain peas according to package directions. In a large glass bowl arrange shredded lettuce on the bottom. The second layer will consist of mixed celery, green pepper and onion. Next, spread peas evenly to make the third layer. Then evenly spread the Miracle Whip over the peas (fourth layer). Sprinkle the sugar over top for the fifth layer. Finally, sprinkle the bacon pieces and then the cheddar cheese on top for the sixth and seventh layers.

Spaghetti Salad

1 lb thin spaghetti
1/2 cucumber, diced
1 bottle of Wishbone Italian salad dressing
2 tomatoes, diced
Salad Supreme by McCormick, 3/4 of the container

Prepare spaghetti according to package directions. Mix the spaghetti with the rest of the ingredients and chill 3-4 hours.

Spinach Salad

1-10 oz pkg fresh spinach
fresh mushrooms sliced
fried bacon, crumbled
water chestnuts, sliced
hard cooked eggs, sliced
green onion, chopped
tomatoes, sliced

Toss ingredients together.

Dressing:
3/4 cup vegetable oil
1/4 cup vinegar
1/4 cup sugar
1 Tbsps dry mustard
1 tsp celery seed
1/2 tsp salt
pepper to taste

Mix and chill. Pour over salad, toss. Top with seeds, peanuts or croutons (my choice).

Taco Salad

1-1/2 lbs. ground beef
1 large onion
1 pkg. taco mix
1/2 cup water
1 large bottle Catalina salad dressing
1 head lettuce torn in bite-sized pieces
2 to 3 tomatoes, chopped
1 cup grated cheddar cheese
1 large bag nacho cheese Doritos

Brown ground beef and onion. Drain. Add taco mix and water, simmer 5 minutes and cool. Layer: tomatoes, lettuce, onion, cheese and meat. Add broken Doritos and salad dressing before serving.

Kim's Deviled Eggs

6 eggs
2 heaping tablespoons mayo
1 tsp. mustard
paprika

Soak eggs in cold water for 15 minutes. Bring to boil, boil for 10 minutes. Take eggs out and let cool. Shell (this should be easy if you followed the above procedure), and halve lengthwise. Carefully lift out yolks and place in mixing bowl. Mash yolks with fork and add mayo and mustard. Mix until fluffy. Fill egg whites with yolk mixture. Sprinkle with paprika.

Brown and Serve Rolls

Fresh home-baked, have-on-hand rolls

1 pkg. active dry yeast
3/4 cup warm water (105 to 115 degrees)
3/4 cup lukewarm milk (scalded then cooled)
1/4 cup sugar
2-1/4 teaspoons salt
1/4 cup shortening
4-1/2 cups all-purpose flour

Dissolve yeast in warm water. Stir in milk, sugar, salt, shortening and 2-1/2 cups of the flour. Beat until smooth. Mix in remaining flour to form soft dough.

Turn dough into lightly floured board; knead until smooth and elastic, about 5 minutes. Place in greased bowl; turn greased side up. Cover; let rise in warm place until double, about 1-1/2 hours.

Punch down dough; turn onto lightly floured board and divide into 24 equal pieces. Shape each piece into smooth ball. Place in greased muffin cups or about 3 inches apart on greased baking sheet. Cover; let rise until almost double, about 45 minutes.

Heat oven to 275 degrees. Bake 20 to 30 minutes (do not allow rolls to brown). Remove from pans and cool at room temperature.

Place rolls in plastic bags or wrap in plastic wrap or aluminum foil. Store in refrigerator for several days or freeze. At serving time, brown rolls in 400 degree oven 7 to 10 minutes.

Stuffing

1 pkg. bread cubes
1 large onion, chopped
3 stalks celery, chopped
2 eggs
Enough water to moisten stuffing
salt and pepper to taste
sage to taste
poultry seasoning to taste

Mix above ingredients together. Use to stuff turkey, chicken or pork.

Fish

Baked Fish

1 lb. fresh or frozen fillets of haddock
1 egg
1/4 cup flour
Salt and pepper to taste
1 tsp. lemon juice
Butter or margarine

Beat egg, dip fish in egg then coat fish with flour, salt and pepper. Squeeze lemon juice over fish and top with pieces of butter or margarine. Bake 350 degrees until golden brown.

Salmon Cakes

1 can Salmon
1 egg
1 onion, minced fine
Salt and pepper to taste
Bread crumbs
Oil or butter for frying

Mix Salmon, egg, onion and seasonings in a bowl. Shape into cakes. Roll each cake in bread crumbs. Fry cakes in oil or butter until golden brown on both sides.

Main Dishes and Vegetables

Fried Chicken

Chicken breasts or a whole cut-up chicken
1 egg
1/2 cup milk
1/2 cup flour
1/4 tsp. paprika
salt and pepper to taste

Beat egg and add milk. Mix flour; paprika, salt and pepper in a separate bowl. Dip chicken in egg mixture and then in flour mixture, coating thoroughly. Fry until golden brown. Drain on paper towels.

Beef Stew

2 lbs. stew beef, cut in small pieces
1 large onion, chopped
1 tsp. garlic powder
3 carrots cut in small pieces
3 potatoes cut in small pieces
1/2 cup flour
1 tsp. Kitchen Bouquet
3 tsp. vegetable oil
1/2 tsp. salt and pepper
1 tsp. Mrs. Dash's
2-3 cups water, enough to make gravy
1 can of peas

Mix together flour, garlic, salt and pepper, and Mrs. Dash's in a zip-lock bag. Add stew beef and coat with mixture. In large skillet put enough vegetable oil to coat bottom of skillet. Add coated stew beef and brown. Add onions and cook until tender. Add water and Kitchen Bouquet to make gravy. Add carrots and potatoes. Cook until potatoes and carrots are tender, about 20 minutes. Add peas and cook 5 minutes more.

Meat Loaf

1/2 cup Italian Bread Crumbs
1/4 cup milk
1-1/2 lbs. ground beef
1 egg, beaten
1/2 cup chopped onion
1 tbsp. Worcestershire sauce
3 tbsp. ketchup
1 tbsp. mustard

1/2 tsp. salt
1/2 tsp. pepper
1 tbsp. finely chopped green pepper

In large mixing bowl, soak bread crumbs in milk for a few minutes. Add the rest of the ingredients and mix well. Shape into a loaf and place in a 9x13 pan. Pour Brown Sugar Tomato Sauce over all. Bake at 250 degrees for 1 hour. After the first 30 minutes, baste often with the sauce in the pan.

Brown Sugar Tomato Sauce

1-1/4 cups tomato sauce
2 tbsp. brown sugar
2 tbsp. vinegar
1/4 cup water

Combine all sauce ingredients together and mix well.

Chili

1 pkg. McCormick Original Chili Seasoning Mix
1 lb. ground beef
1 onion chopped
1 large can kidney beans
2 cans Hunt's stewed tomatoes
1 can Hunt's tomato sauce
 Chili powder to taste

Brown meat and onion; combine other ingredients. Simmer for 30 minutes.

Chopped Suey

1-1/2 lbs. pork, cut in small pieces
1 tablespoon vegetable oil
1 onion, chopped
2 cups celery, chopped
1 can La Choy bean sprouts
1 can La Choy vegetables
1-1/2 teaspoons soy sauce
1 can La Choy noodles
2-3 tablespoons cornstarch mixed with 2-3 tablespoons water

In large skillet, add vegetable oil, add pork; stir-fry 2 minutes or until pork is no longer pink. Stir in remaining ingredients, except noodles. Heat to boiling. Stir in cornstarch mixture. Cook till thickened. Serve over noodles or rice.

Corned Beef Hash

1 can corned beef
5 or 6 potatoes
1 large onion
Dash of Mrs. Dash's
Salt and pepper to taste
2 to 3 tbsp. butter

In a large skillet combine all ingredients and cook over medium heat for 30 minutes.

Poppy's Corn Fritters

Make pancake **batter using** directions on box. Add whole, or cream **style corn** (drained). Drop two or three tablespoons on a **hot** skillet. Cook until golden brown on both sides. Serve **with** butter and syrup.

Creamed Chipped Beef

1 or 2 pkgs. chipped beef
2 tablespoons butter or margarine
1-tablespoon flour
About 1 cup milk

Melt butter or margarine in medium fry pan. Add chipped beef and sauté. Add flour, stir until mixed together, then add milk. Stir 1 minute. Serve over toast.

Egg Fu Young

1 large can shrimp drained or 1 lb fresh shrimp
1 can bean sprouts drained
1/2 cup celery, thinly sliced
1/4 cup onions, thinly sliced
6 eggs
Salt & pepper to taste
1 tbsp. soy sauce
Heinz Beef Gravy with Mushrooms

Combine all ingredients except eggs and mix thoroughly. Add eggs to mixture and blend together. Heat enough oil to cover bottom of a large skillet. Form patties using approximately 1/3 cup of mixture. Fry until brown on both sides turning only once. Heat a jar of Heinz beef gravy with mushrooms in small saucepan. Pour over patties and serve hot.

Grilled Cheese and Tomato Soup

4 slices white bread (can use wheat bread)
Butter or margarine
8 slices American cheese
1 can tomato soup
2/3 can milk (not water)

Put butter or margarine on both sides of bread and place 2 slices, butter side down, in skillet. Put 2 slices of cheese on each slice of bread and put the other 2 slices of bread on top with the butter or margarine side up. Brown on both sides. Mix tomato soup and milk together and heat till hot. 2 servings.

Ham and Cabbage

Ham bone with a good amount of ham on it.
1 large head of cabbage, cut in quarters
4 or 5 potatoes, peeled and cut in half
salt and pepper to taste
enough water to cover

Mix all of the above ingredients in a large pot and cook until the potatoes are tender, about 30 minutes.

Leftover cabbage is delicious fried the next day.

Hamburgers

1 lb. lean ground beef
1 egg
1 onion, finely chopped
1/4 tsp. garlic

Mix together and shape into patties. Cook in frying pan, turning once.

Lasagne

1 lb. Italian sausage
1 lb. ground beef
1 clove garlic, minced
1 onion
Spaghetti sauce (see spaghetti sauce recipe)
1 tsp. salt
Wide lasagna noodles
3 cups cream-style cottage cheese
1/2 cup grated Parmesan cheese
1 lb. mozzarella cheese thinly sliced

Brown meat, drain grease. Add garlic and spaghetti sauce, simmer for 10 minutes, stirring occasionally. Cook noodles in boiling, salted water until tender. Drain and rinse in cold water. Place a layer of noodles in a 9x13-inch baking dish. Spread some of the cheeses then some of the spaghetti sauce. Repeat in layers. End with sauce and cheese on top. Bake at 350 for 30 minutes.

Italian Potatoes

4 large baking potatoes, peeled and diced into 1/2 inch chunks
3 large sweet potatoes, peeled and cut into 1/2 inch chunks
1 large onion, finely chopped
1/2 cup fresh parsley, finely chopped
4 cloves garlic, minced
1/4 cup olive oil
1 tsp salt
1 tsp. Italian seasoning
1/2 tsp. ground black pepper

Mix together all of the above. Toss well to thoroughly coat potatoes. Place in baking pan (preferably rectangular so the potatoes are not stacked on top of each other and they can brown a bit). Bake at 350 degrees for about 45 minutes (covered with foil). Check potatoes, mix well, uncover and bake an additional one-half hour or so until potatoes are tender. Do not over brown.

Mashed Potatoes

5 lbs. potatoes
1 stick butter or margarine
1/4 cup milk (or less if preferred)
Salt and pepper to taste

Boil potatoes until tender. Mash with electric mixer. Add butter or margarine and salt and pepper. Gradually, add milk, beating until light and fluffy.

Left Over Mashed Potatoes

Potato Cakes

Shape potatoes into patties, coat frying pan with butter or margarine, and fry patties until golden brown.

Potatoes with Cheese

Put potatoes in individual aluminum foil cups. Bake till hot. Top with either grated sharp cheddar cheese or top with American cheese. Return to oven until cheese is melted.

Potatoes with Good Seasons Italian Dressing

4 lbs. red potatoes, sliced or cut in cubes
1 package Good Seasons Italian dressing
(and oil and vinegar to make)

Preheat oven to 350 degrees. Cook potatoes until tender. Arrange in oblong baking dish. Mix Good Seasons Italian dressing according to directions on envelope and pour over potatoes. Let set until ready to bake. Bake until warm and tops are lightly brown, about 20 minutes.

Scalloped Potatoes

4 potatoes
1/2 cup diced onion
1/4 cup celery
1 tbsp. parsley
3 tbsp. flour
1 tbsp. butter
1-1/2 tsp. salt
1/2 tsp. pepper
1-1/2 cups milk
2 cups grated sharp cheese

Peel potatoes, cook slightly, and slice. Place in buttered 2-quart casserole. Combine remaining ingredients, except cheese, in blender. Pour mixture over potatoes. Top with cheese. Bake at 250 for 1 hour.

Spaghetti Sauce

2 pkgs. Lawry's Spaghetti Sauce Mix.
1 lb. ground beef
1 can Hunt's tomato sauce
2 cans Hunt's stewed tomatoes
1 onion
Mrs. Dash's
Brown ground beef, onion and a sprinkle of Mrs. Dash's. Drain and add other ingredients and simmer for 30 minutes.

Stewed Tomatoes

In a medium sauce pan combine:
1 can tomatoes (crushed up)
1 slice bread (cubed)
Sugar to taste or 6 pkgs. Splenda
Heat and serve over mashed potatoes, corn beef hash, or on buttered bread.

Sweet and Sour Meat Balls

Make meat balls with ground beef and brown in a little oil.

Sweet and Sour Sauce

6 slices fresh ginger root
1 clove garlic, chopped
4 green onions (2-inch pieces)
1 green pepper, cuit into cubes
1 small oinion, cut into cubes
6 tbsp. catsup
3/4 cup vinegar
1 cup sugar
4 tbsp. Worcestershire sauce
2 tbsp. cornstarch, mixed with 2 tbsp. water

Pour some oil into a saucepan over medium heat; add garlic, onions, ginger root and green pepper. Stir-fry 1 minute. Add catsup, sugar and Worcestershire sauce. Cook 1 minute. Add vinegar. Stir until sugar is dissolved. Gradually pour in cornstarch mixture; stir constantly unitl thick.

Add Meat Balls. You may freeze until ready to use.

Swiss Steak

3 tbsp. all-purpose flour
1/2 tsp. salt
1/2 tsp. pepper
Dash of Mrs. Dash's
2 cloves garlic, finely chopped or garlic powder
1 1/2 lbs. Beef-boneless round or sirloin steak
2 tbsp. vegetable oil
1 can Hunt's tomato sauce
1 cup water
1 large onion chopped
1 large green bell pepper, sliced (optional)
1/4 tsp. Kitchen Bouquet Seasoning Sauce

Mix flour, salt, pepper, and Mrs. Dash's in zip lock bag and coat steak.
Brown in large pan with vegetable oil. Add garlic and onion, cook 1 minute. Add water and Kitchen Bouquet to make gravy. Add tomato sauce and green bell pepper. Simmer for 45 minutes.

Casseroles

Baked Macaroni and Cheese

1 lb. elbow macaroni
3 cups shredded sharp cheddar cheese
3-4 slices American cheese
2 cups milk
1/2 stick butter or margarine

Cook macaroni according to package directions until barely tender; drain and run cold water over macaroni. In a 9x13 inch casserole, add in layers: macaroni, cheese, butter and milk. Sprinkle sharp cheddar cheese on top. Bake at 350 degrees for about 15 minutes.

Chicken and Broccoli Casserole

Broccoli florets, cooked
Chicken breasts, cooked
1 can cream of mushroom soup
1/2 cup mayonnaise or Miracle Whip
4-6 slices American cheese
1 can French fried onions

Preheat oven to 350 degrees. Combine the cream of mushroom soup and mayonnaise. In a baking dish, layer the chicken, broccoli, and cheese. Spoon the soup mixture over the cheese. Sprinkle the onions over all and bake for about 20 minutes.

Potato Casserole

2 packages (30 ounces each) country-style hash browns, thawed
3/4 cup butter, melted, divided
4 cups (32 ounces) sour cream
2 cans (10-3/4 ounces each) condensed cream of chicken soup, undiluted
1 bunch green onions, sliced
4 cups (16 ounces) shredded cheddar cheese
1 teaspoon salt
1/4 teaspoon pepper
1-1/2 cups cornflakes, crushed

In large bowl, combine the potatoes, 1/2 cup butter, sour cream, soup, onions, cheese, salt and pepper. Transfer to two greased, shallow, 3-quart baking dishes.

Combine cornflakes and remaining butter, sprinkle evenly over tops. Bake uncovered, at 350 degrees for 55-60 minutes or until bubbly. Yield: 26-30 servings.

Ragu Casserole

1-1/2 lbs ground beef
1 onion
2 garlic cloves, minced (or garlic powder)
salt and pepper to taste
1 jar Ragu spaghetti mix
2 cups grated sharp cheddar cheese
1 box elbow macaroni

Cook macaroni until tender. Drain. Brown ground beef, onion, garlic, salt and pepper. Drain. In 9x13 inch dish add all ingredients except cheese. Sprinkle cheese on top and bake 50 degrees for 25 minutes.

Shepherd's Pie

1-1/2 lbs ground beef
2 cloves garlic, chopped or garlic powder
salt and pepper to taste
4 cups mashed potatoes
1 pkg. mixed frozen vegetables
1 cup leftover gravy (or 1 cup ready made gravy)

Brown ground beef, add garlic, onion and salt and pepper, cook 2 minutes longer. Drain and put in 2-quart casserole. Add gravy and vegetables. Spoon potatoes over top. Bake uncovered at 350 degrees for 20 minutes.

Sweet Potato Casserole

3 cups mashed sweet potatoes or vacuum packed can (18 oz.)
1/8 cup sugar
1 stick butter
2 eggs
1 tsp. vanilla

Mix above ingredients together until smooth.
Put in baking dish.

Mix together and spread over above:

1 cup brown sugar
1/3 cup butter
1/3 cup flour

Top with 1 cup chopped pecans.

Bake at 350 for 30 minutes.

Fruits and Desserts

Ambrosia

1 large can fruit cocktail (drained)
1 medium can pineapple tidbits (drained)
1 can mandarin oranges (drained)
1 cup mini marshmallows
1 cup coconut
Maraschino cherries (optional)
Mix with 8 oz. Cool whip

Refrigerate and serve.

Apple Sauce

2 pounds apples
1 teaspoons cinnamon
1 teaspoon nutmeg
1-1/2 teaspoons lemon juice
enough water to cover apples

Peel and core apples and cut in quarters. Add cinnamon, nutmeg, lemon juice and water. Bring to a boil. Simmer until apples are tender. Leave in chunks or simmer till smooth

If using Golden Delicious or McIntosh apples you won't need sugar. If you use Granny Smith you will need to add a little sugar.

Nanny Hazel's Applesauce Cake

2-1/2 cups sifted all-purpose flour
1-3/4 cups sugar
1/4 tsp. baking powder
1 tsp. cinnamon
1-1/2 tsp. baking soda
1-1/2 tsp. salt
1/2 tsp. each of cloves, all spice, and nutmeg
1/2 cup shortening
1-15 oz. can applesauce
3 eggs
1 cup seedless raisins
1 cup finely chopped walnuts

Grease and flour bunt pan. Sift dry ingredients. Add shortening and applesauce. Add eggs. Beat 2 minutes with electric mixer. Combine raisins and walnuts with rubber scraper. Bake in 350 degree oven for 45 minutes.

Chocolate Chip Cake
(50th Wedding anniversary cake)

1 box yellow or white cake mix
4 eggs
1 cup water
1 box vanilla instant pudding
1/2 cup oil
About 1/2 cup chocolate chips, ground in a food processor

Filling

1 8-ounce brick cream cheese, softened
1 can sweetened condensed milk
1 tsp. vanilla
1/3 cup lemon juice
About 1/2 cup chocolate chips, ground in a food processor
1 can Duncan Hines prepared chocolate frosting

Preheat oven to 350 degrees. Combine all the cake ingredients until well blended. Pour into prepared cake pans. Bake for 30 minutes. Remove from oven when toothpick inserted in center comes out clean and allow to cool. Meanwhile, prepare filling by blending cream cheese, condensed milk, vanilla, lemon juice, and ground chocolate chips together. When cake is cool, spread filling in between cake layers. Frost with prepared Duncan Hines prepared frosting. This cake must be refrigerated to prevent spoilage.

"To-Die-For" Chocolate Fudge

3 cups sugar
1 cup heavy cream
4 tablespoons unsweetened cocoa powder
1 tablespoon light corn syrup
1 tablespoon unsalted butter, softened
1 teaspoon vanilla extract

Place the sugar, cream, cocoa and corn syrup in a saucepan and heat over low heat, stirring constantly until smooth. Keep fudge mixture on enough heat to get it to start to bubble (don't let it start to boil – it should just bubble). Take a teaspoon tip's worth of the fudge mixture and drop it into a cup of water. If the fudge forms a soft ball instead of melting into the water, the fudge is ready for the next step. Remove the fudge from the heat and gently stir in the butter. Stir well, to incorporate the butter throughout. Add the vanilla extract while stirring. Pour the fudge into a pre-buttered baking dish (9x9 inch pan). Set on a rack and let cool. When cooled and hardened, cut into squares.

Cranberry Cheese Ribbon Mold

1 envelope unflavored gelatin
1 cup cold water
1 (3 oz.) pkg. strawberry Jell-o
3/4 cup boiling water
1 (14 oz.) jar cranberry-orange relish
1/4 cup lemon juice
1 tsp. grated rind
1 (8 oz.) pkg. cream cheese
1 (4-1/2 oz.) container cool whip

In a pan, sprinkle unflavored gelatin over the cold water; heat until dissolved and set aside. Dissolve strawberry Jello in boiling water. Combine relish and 2 teaspoons lemon and orange rind. Put into mold and leave until set. Beat cream cheese with the rest of the lemon; fold in Cool Whip. Add unflavored Jell-o and mix well. Spoon over Jell-o mixture and cool well.

Ice Cream Lime Parfait Pie
(Or as Kim remembers it: Lime "Parkway" Pie)

9-inch baked pastry shell or graham cracker crust
2 boxes lime Jell-o
2 cups water
1 qt. vanilla ice cream
Whipped cream

Bake pastry shell or graham cracker crust as directed. Cool.
Dissolve gelatin in boiling water. Stir in ice cream until melted.
Pour into pie shell. Chill 2 hours or until served.
Serve topped with whipped cream.

Lemon Meringue Pie

Filling
3 boxes lemon pie filling
1 1/2 cups sugar
3/4 cup water + six cups water
6 egg yolks

2 pastry crusts or ready-made crusts

Put all filling ingredients in a large saucepan. Add six cups of water and stir constantly over medium heat until it comes to a full boil. Pour filling into two cooled pie crusts.

Meringue
6 egg whites
1 cup sugar
1 pinch of cream of tartar

Beat six egg whites until foamy; gradually add 1 cup sugar and a pinch of cream of tartar. Beat until peaks are high and glossy. Pile onto cold pie filling and use a spoon to swirl to outer edges and to make peaks. Place in hot oven (350) just until tips are lightly browned. Two minutes at most, watch carefully!

Will make two 9-inch pies.

Orange Delight Cake

1 pkg. yellow cake mix
4 eggs
1/2 cup oil
1 can mandarin oranges with juice

Mix together ingredients and pour into three 9x12 inch cake pans. Bake for 30 minutes at 325. Cool completely. Fill and frost with the following frosting recipe.

Frosting

1 (12 OZ.) Cool Whip
1 pkg. vanilla instant pudding
1 medium can crushed pineapple with juice

Combine all above ingredients and frost cake. Refrigerate leftovers.

Orange Pineapple Mold

1 (16 oz.) pkg. Orange Jell-o
2 cups boiling water
1 (15 oz.) can crushed pineapple
1 qt. vanilla ice cream
1 can drained mandarin oranges

Dissolve Jell-o in 2 cups boiling water; fold in crushed pineapple. Add ice cream and mandarin oranges. Use a 6-cup mold. Sets in about an hour.

Peanut Butter Fudge

1 cup margarine
1 pkg. 12 oz. Chocolate chips
1 pound crunchy peanut butter
1 box (16 oz.) powdered sugar

Melt margarine and chocolate chips in microwave, stir in peanut butter and powdered sugar. Pour into greased 9x13 inch dish. Chill and cut into squares.
Yield 70 squares.

Rocky Road Fudge Bars

1/2 cup butter or margarine
1 square or envelope (1 oz.) unsweetened chocolate
1 cup sugar
1 cup Pillsbury flour
1/2 cup chopped nuts
1 teaspoon baking powder
1 teaspoon vanilla
2 eggs

Filling

6 oz. cream cheese, softened
1/2 cup sugar
2 tablespoons flour
1/4 cup butter or margarine, softened
1 egg
1/2 teaspoon vanilla
1/4 cup chopped nuts

Frosting

2 cups miniature marshmallows
1/4 cup butter or margarine
1 square or envelope (1 oz.) unsweetened chocolate
2 oz. cream cheese
1/4 cup milk
1 lb. (about 3 cups) powdered sugar
1 teaspoon vanilla

Preheat oven to 350. In large saucepan, melt butter and chocolate over low heat; remove from heat. Add sugar, flour, nuts, baking powder, vanilla and eggs; mix well. Spread in greased and floured 13x9 inch pan. In bowl, combine filling ingredients; spread over chocolate mixture in pan. Bake 25 to 35 minutes or until toothpick inserted in center comes out clean. Sprinkle with marshmallows and bake 2 minutes longer. Immediately prepare frosting by combining butter, chocolate, cream cheese and milk in saucepan. Heat over low heat until chocolate melts. Stir in powdered sugar and vanilla until smooth. Pour over marshmallows and swirl together. Cool and cut into 36 bars.

Strawberry Dip

1 jar marshmallow fluff
1 container strawberry cream cheese

Mix with electric mixer until smooth. Serve with strawberries.

Recipe Index

Soups, Salads, Breads 7

Duke's Favorite Bean Soup 8
Clam Chowder 9
Vegetable Soup 10
Yummy Baked Beans 11
Cole Slaw 12
Corn Pudding 12
Flemion Salad 13
Manhattan Deli Salad 13
Picnic Pineapple Slaw 14
Potato Salad 14
Seven Layer Salad 15
Spaghetti Salad 16
Spinach Salad 17
Taco Salad 18
Kim's Deviled Eggs 19
Brown and Serve Rolls 20
Stuffing 21

Fish 22

Baked Fish 23
Salmon Cakes 23

Main Dishes and Vegetables 24

Fried Chicken 25
Beef Stew 26
Meat Loaf 27
Chili 28
Chopped Suey 29
Corned Beef Hash 30
Poppy's Corn Fritters 30
Creamed Chipped Beef 31
Egg Fu Young 31
Grilled Cheese and Tomato Soup 32
Ham and Cabbage 32
Hamburgers 33
Lasagne 33
Italian Potatoes 34
Mashed Potatoes 34
Potato Cakes 35
Potatoes with Cheese 35
Potatoes with Good Seasons Italian Dressing 35
Scalloped Potatoes 36
Spaghetti Sauce 37
Stewed Tomatoes 37
Sweet and Sour Meatballs 38
Swiss Steak 39

Casseroles 40

Baked Macaroni and Cheese 41
Chicken and Broccoli Casserole 41
Potato Casserole 42
Ragu Casserole 43
Shepherd's Pie 43
Sweet Potato Casserole 44

Fruits and Desserts 45

Ambrosia 46
Apple Sauce 46
Nanny Hazel's Applesauce Cake 47
Chocolate Chip Cake 48
"To-Die-For" Chocolate Fudge 49
Cranberry Cheese Ribbon Mold 50
Ice Cream Lime Parfait Pie 51
Lemon Meringue Pie 52
Orange Delight Cake 53
Orange Pineapple Mold 53
Peanut Butter Fudge 54
Rocky Road Fudge Bars 54
Strawberry Dip 55

Printed in the United States
128968LV00002B/1/P